Science
STARTS

SEEDS GO, SEEDS GROW

by Mark Weakland

CAPSTONE PRESS
a capstone imprint

Hard and silent, a seed
does not look alive.

2

But inside each seed is a living plant waiting to grow.

Every seed has a tough outside coat. The coat keeps the small living part of the seed safe.

4

Beneath the coat, a layer of food feeds the seed as it grows.

5

Where can you find seeds? Everywhere!

Fleshy fruits like watermelons and pumpkins hold handfuls of seeds.

Some seeds, like sunflower seeds, are easy to see. They grow on the outside of a plant.

seeds

Peas are seeds that grow inside pods.

10

The outside of each pea will dry up and harden until planting time.

Seeds from a maple tree twirl through the air like helicopters.

Dandelion seeds drift in the wind like balloons, traveling to faraway places.

13

A coconut seed floats like a boat
in the water. Carried by ocean
currents, it lands on a beach.
Then the seed will sprout.

Prickly seeds covered in hooks stick to the fur of animals.

Carried by dogs, bears, and other furry creatures, these seeds hitch a ride to a new location.

How are seeds made?
They begin with flowers.
Each flower produces pollen.
Grains of pollen look like
fuzzy yellow dust near the
center of a flower.

Busy butterflies, bees, and moths carry pollen from blossom to blossom. This process is called pollination.

After pollen grains attach to the sticky insides of a flower, seeds begin to form. As the seeds grow larger, the old flower falls away.

Most seeds fall to the earth and grow without help. People sometimes help seeds to grow by planting them in the soil.

When seeds get warm enough and plenty of water, they awaken.

The seed bursts out of its shell coat and begins to grow, or germinate. Roots push into the soil.

Planted seeds cast off their shell coats. They become seedlings.

What was once a hard seed is
now a soft green plant.

Glossary

current—moving water that flows faster than the rest of the water

fleshy—soft and thick

germinate—to grow out of a seed

pod—a long case that holds the seeds of certain plants, such as peas

pollen—tiny, yellow grains in flowers

pollination—moving pollen from flower to flower; pollination helps flowers make seeds

seedling—a young plant that has just sprouted from a seed

Read More

Bodach, Vijaya Khisty. *Seeds*. Plant Parts. Mankato, Minn.: Capstone Press, 2007.

Macken, JoAnn Early. *Flip, Float, Fly!: Seeds on the Move*. New York: Holiday House, 2008.

Orme, Helen. *Seeds, Bulbs, Plants & Flowers*. Science Everywhere! Mankato, Minn.: NewForest Press, 2011.

Internet SITES

FactHound offers a safe, fun way to find Internet sites related to this book. All of the sites on FactHound have been researched by our staff.

Here's all you do:

Visit *www.facthound.com*

Type in this code: 9781429652520

Check out projects, games and lots more at www.capstonekids.com

Index

A+ Books are published by Capstone Press,
1710 Roe Crest Drive,
North Mankato, MN 56003.
www.capstonepub.com

Library of Congress Cataloging-in-Publication Data
Weakland, Mark.
  Seeds go, seeds grow / by Mark Weakland.
    p. cm.—(A+ books. Science starts)
  Includes bibliographical references and index.
  Summary: "Simple text and photographs explain the basic science behind seeds"—Provided by publisher.
    ISBN 978-1-4296-5252-0 (library binding)—ISBN 978-1-4296-6145-4 (paperback)
    1. Seeds—Juvenile literature. I. Title.
    QK661.W38 2011
      581.4'67—dc22

                              2010038877

Credits
  Jenny Marks, editor; Alison Thiele, designer; Marcie Spence, media researcher; Eric Manske, production specialist

Photo Credits
  Alamy Images: Scott Camazine, 16-17; iStockphoto: cjp, 24-25, fotobaby, 22-23, IgorDutina, 2-3, imv, 13, kkgas, 1, OGphoto, 12;
Science Photo Library: Steve Percival, cover; Shutterstock: Ales Studeny, 10-11, Anna Sedneva, 4-5, Filipe B. Varela, 28, fotohunter, 6-7,
Gorilla, 20-21, Marie C. Fields, 18-19, R-photos, 29, Richard Griffin, 27, Smit, 26, tomas del amo, 14-15, Yuriy Kulyk, 8-9

Note to Parents, Teachers, and Librarians
The Science Starts series supports national education standards related to science. This book describes and illustrates seeds. The images support early readers in understanding the text. The repetition of words and phrases helps early readers learn new words. This book also introduces early readers to subject-specific vocabulary words, which are defined in the Glossary section. Early readers may need assistance to read some words and to use the Table of Contents, Glossary, Read More, Internet Sites, and Index sections of the book.

Printed in the United States   4843